SUPERDADS!

I'm scared!

Have no fear.
Your superdads
are here!

cowritten by
HEATHER LANG and JAMIE HARPER

illustrated by JAMIE HARPER

CANDLEWICK PRESS

Bringing up babies in the wild is a mighty big job. Animal moms usually get the credit since they're the ones who do most of the parenting. But some dads take the lead and even risk their lives for their families!

Who are these unsung heroes who care for their young in unique and surprising ways?

Some superdads are incredible incubators, providing safe and healthy environments in which their young can grow.

A brown kiwi dad is in charge of egg-sitting.

He keeps his developing chicks toasty warm for up to eighty days.

A mallee fowl dad designs a volcano-shaped nest layered with leaves and sand. He checks the temperature frequently with his built-in beak thermometer and adds or removes sand if necessary.

Incubation is a tough workout for a giant water bug dad. With up to 150 eggs stuck to his back, he does push-ups to keep oxygen flowing over them.

A seahorse dad carries his fry in his pouch . . . until it's time to give birth.

Did you hear the news?

He's pregnant!

Honey, you've never looked better!

Are you my mom?

Hope he has enough names.

A Darwin's frog dad carries his tadpoles in his throat. And when they turn into froglets . . . he "burps" them up.

Superdads work super hard to house and hide their young.

A baya weaver dad uses his excellent engineering skills to attract a mate and make a home for his future chicks. He ties together hundreds of strips of leaves and grasses using only his beak.

A sungrebe dad keeps his chicks in secret compartments underneath his wings.

A three-spined stickleback dad makes a hidden nest step-by-step.

He digs a pit,

collects vegetation,

and sticks everything together

with a gluey substance he squirts out his back end.

Once he shapes it into a dome,

he constructs the tunnel.

I love this part.

WHAM!

WHAM!
WHAM!

Ta-da!

When it's feeding time, superdads know how to get the job done.

I call the front seat!

For a golden lion tamarin dad, it's double trouble! He finds and prepares food with two babies in tow.

Yum, a new fruit!

No bugs today?

A burying beetle dad finds and buries a dead animal for his newborns to feast on. Yummy!

He also spits up nutritious goodies for them to eat.

A sandgrouse dad flies long distances across the desert to find water. He drenches his feathers and then races back to feed his thirsty chicks.

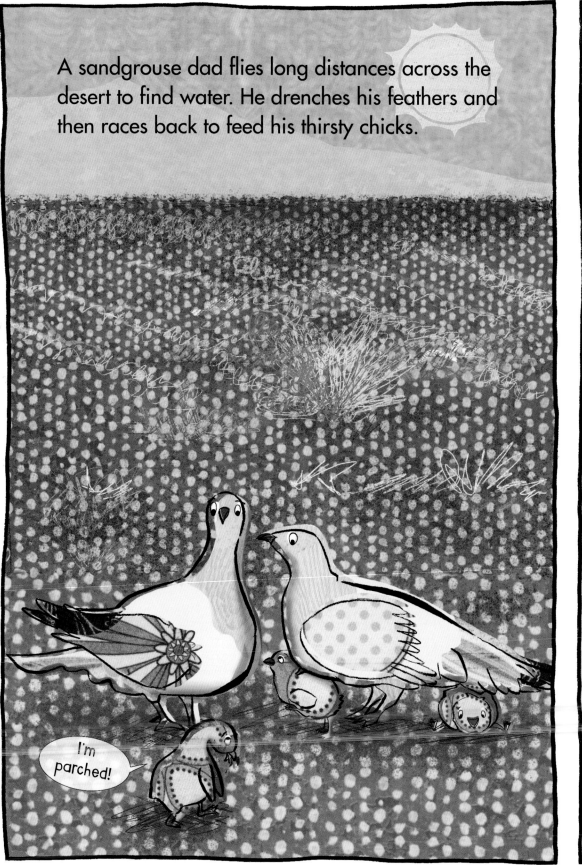

Fear not! Superdads are fierce protectors.

You don't have to be big to be brave! A tiny glass frog dad uses powerful kicks to defend his eggs against predators.

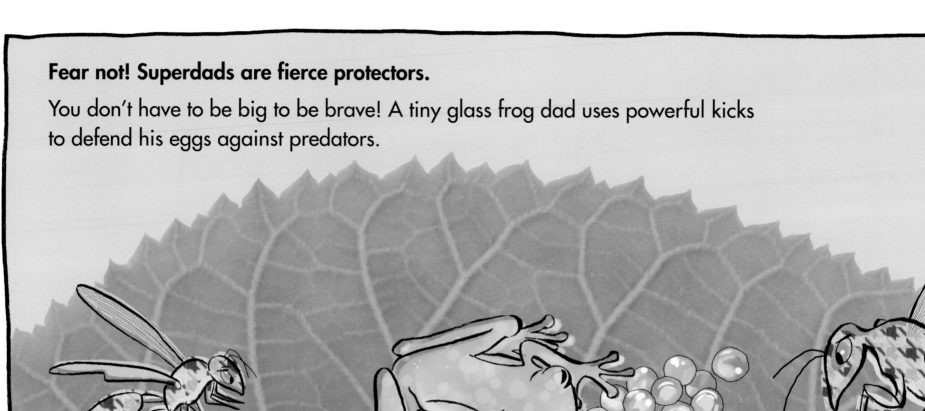

An African bullfrog dad's enemy is the hot sun. If his tadpoles' pool starts to dry out, he leaps into action, digging a trench to a new water source.

When it comes to single dads, the greater rhea takes the prize! He cares for and protects his humongous brood 24–7.

Who says learning can't be fun! Superdads make time to play and in the process teach their babies important life skills.

A gorilla dad makes the perfect jungle gym.

THUMP!

An owl monkey dad plays follow-the-leader with his young.

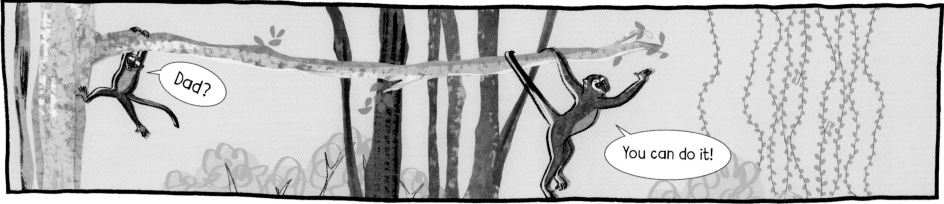

A wolf dad plays tug-of-war . . . .

Tickle, tickle, tickle.

and ambush!

Now, where did he go?

OwOOO

I got you!

Bringing up babies in the wild is a mighty big job! But these superdads, whether huge or teeny-tiny, are always ready for the challenge. Devoted, hardworking, fierce, and fun, they go above and beyond to raise offspring who will someday be super, too.

BROWN KIWI
SUPER PATIENT

I LIVE in New Zealand's forests and grasslands, and I EAT earthworms, snails, insects, and fruit.

GUESS WHAT? My long beak has nostrils on the end and is ideal for sniffing out dinner.

MALLEE FOWL
SUPER SCIENTIFIC

I LIVE in dry areas of Australia, and I EAT wattle seeds, flower blossoms, buds, fruit, and insects.

GUESS WHAT? I keep my nest at just the right temperature (about 92°F/33°C) by adding or removing leaf litter and sand.

He's such a nerd!

GIANT WATER BUG
SUPER ATHLETIC

We need flippers!

And a noodle too!

I LIVE in freshwater ponds, lakes, and wetlands, and I EAT other insects, snails, tadpoles, small fish, and frogs.

GUESS WHAT? On my rear end, I have a snorkel-like tube, which I breathe through when I'm underwater.

SEAHORSE
SUPER UNIQUE

I LIVE in tropical and temperate shallow coastal waters, and I EAT tiny shrimp, plankton, and algae.

GUESS WHAT? Unlike other fish, I don't have a tail fin, so I swim up-right using the tiny fin on my back.

DARWIN'S FROG
SUPER CAREFUL

I LIVE along forest streams, and I EAT insects, worms, and snails.

GUESS WHAT? If I'm in danger, I'll hop into the water and play dead. Floating on my back, I look just like a leaf.

BAYA WEAVER
SUPER TALENTED

I LIVE in grasslands, scrublands, and fields, and I EAT seeds and insects.

GUESS WHAT? It may take me 500 trips and up to 18 days to collect my nest materials.

Could you make me a game room?

SUNGREBE
SUPER SECRETIVE

I LIVE in slow-flowing streams with lots of vegetation, and I EAT snails, small fish, frogs, seeds, and fruit.

GUESS WHAT? My chicks hatch after only 10 to 11 days, so they're born underdeveloped and helpless.

THREE-SPINED STICKLEBACK
SUPER FOCUSED

I LIVE in the sea, estuaries, and fresh water, and I EAT invertebrates and small fish.

GUESS WHAT? If any of my fry escape from the nest, I chase them down, suck them into my mouth, and spit them back into the nest.

Meanie!

GOLDEN LION TAMARIN
SUPER CAPABLE

I LIVE in Brazilian tropical rain forests, and I EAT fruit, bird eggs, insects, and small vertebrates.

GUESS WHAT? I guide my young to hidden prey by calling them with a chattering sound.

BURYING BEETLE
SUPER SKILLED

"SO COOL, Dad!"

I LIVE in open fields, grasslands, and forests, and I EAT dead animals, including birds, fish, and mammals.

GUESS WHAT? After removing the hair from a dead animal, I cover it with special fluid from my mouth and rear end to keep it fresh.

GREAT HORNED OWL
SUPER STEALTHY

I LIVE in forests, deserts, wetlands, backyards, and cities, and I EAT mice, squirrels, rabbits, ducks, reptiles, amphibians, insects, and fish.

GUESS WHAT? I can turn my head almost all the way around, which helps me find prey without making a sound.

SANDGROUSE
SUPER RELIABLE

"I'm parched!"

I LIVE in deserts and dry grasslands, and I EAT seeds and other plant matter.

GUESS WHAT? It can take me up to 15 minutes to fill up my feathers with water to feed my chicks.

GLASS FROG
SUPER NIMBLE

I LIVE in trees along rivers and streams, and I EAT spiders and small insects, including crickets and moths.

GUESS WHAT? My toe pads work like suction cups—perfect for climbing slippery plants.

AFRICAN BULLFROG
SUPER BULLISH

I LIVE in savannas, shrublands, lakes, and marshes, and I EAT insects, small rodents, reptiles, fish, and other amphibians.

GUESS WHAT? I have a spade-shaped knob on my hind feet, which helps me dig.

GREATER RHEA
SUPER VIGILANT

"Can't a chick have some alone time?"

I LIVE mostly in the grasslands of South America, and I EAT plants, fruit, seeds, insects, small reptiles, and rodents.

GUESS WHAT? If my chicks wander off, I follow their loud whistles and clap my beak to call to them.

OWL MONKEY
SUPER LOYAL

I LIVE in forests, and I EAT fruit, flowers, insects, nectar, and leaves.

GUESS WHAT? I not only take care of my little ones; I stick with my mate for life!

GORILLA
SUPER TOLERANT

"Tickle, tickle, tickle."

I LIVE in African rain forests, and I EAT leaves, stems, roots, fruit, and seeds.

GUESS WHAT? I like to snuggle and play, even with babies who aren't my own.

WOLF
SUPER FUN

I LIVE in forests, inland wetlands, grasslands, pastures, and mountains, and I EAT hoofed animals, such as moose, deer, and elk.

GUESS WHAT? I'm always up for wolf games—my thick fur and tough skin protect me well.

Dig in to learn more!

CHILDREN'S BOOKS

Birkhead, Tim. *What It's Like to Be a Bird*. Illustrated by Catherine Rayner. New York: Walker, 2012.

Butterworth, Chris. *Sea Horse: The Shyest Fish in the Sea*. Illustrated by John Lawrence. Somerville, MA: Candlewick, 2006.

Crump, Marty. *The Mystery of Darwin's Frog*. Illustrated by Steve Jenkins and Edel Rodriguez. Honesdale, PA: Boyds Mills, 2013.

Davey, Owen. *Fanatical About Frogs*. London: Flying Eye Books, 2018.

Gianferrari, Maria. *Play Like an Animal!* Illustrated by Mia Powell. Minneapolis: Millbrook, 2020.

Gibbons, Gail. *Gorillas*. New York: Holiday House, 2021.

Jenkins, Steve. *The Beetle Book*. Boston: Houghton Mifflin Harcourt, 2012.

Leaf, Christina. *Great Horned Owls*. Minneapolis: Bellwether Media, 2015.

Markle, Sandra. *The Great Monkey Rescue: Saving the Golden Lion Tamarins*. Minneapolis: Millbrook, 2016.

Marsh, Laura. *Wolves*. Washington, DC: National Geographic Kids, 2012.

ONLINE RESOURCES

"The Banished Beetle Project." Oklahoma State University, Insect Adventure. http://insectadventure.okstate.edu/american-burying-beetle/.

Dian Fossey Gorilla Fund. https://www.gorillafund.org.

International Wolf Center. https://wolf.org.

"Kiwi." San Diego Zoo. https://animals.sandiegozoo.org/animals/kiwi.

National Malleefowl Recovery Team. https://www.nationalmalleefowl.com.au/about/malleefowl-facts/.

Owl Research Institute. https://www.owlresearchinstitute.org/.

"Reticulated Glass Frog." National Geographic Kids. https://kids.nationalgeographic.com/animals/amphibians/facts/reticulatedglassfrog.

The Seahorse Trust. https://www.theseahorsetrust.org/.

AUDIOVISUAL RESOURCES

"Animal Homes: Cities," "Animal Homes: Location, Location, Location," and "Animal Homes: The Nest." Season 33, episodes 11–13, of *Nature*. Produced by Ann Johnson Prum. PBS, 2015.

Animals at Play. Seasons 1–2. Directed by Dan Perowne. Smithsonian, 2019.

"Big Birds Can't Fly." Season 34, episode 3, of *Nature*. Produced and directed by Mike Birkhead. PBS, 2015.

"Fabulous Frogs." Season 32, episode 19, of *Nature*. Produced and directed by Sally Thomson. PBS, 2014.

Owls: Masters of the Night. Directed by Doclights. Doclights, 2020.

AUTHORS' WEBSITES

Visit heatherlangbooks.com and jamieharper.com for additional resources and activities, including links to videos of superdads in action and information about other sources we used to research this book.

ACKNOWLEDGMENTS

We are grateful to the following experts for helping us verify facts and gain new insights into superdads: Ian Magill, research assistant, CBDM Lab, Harvard Medical School; Alison M. Bell, professor and stickleback researcher, Department of Evolution, Ecology, and Behavior, University of Illinois at Urbana-Champaign; Rebecca Kilner, professor of evolutionary biology, University of Cambridge; Marc Bekoff, animal behavior researcher and professor emeritus of ecology and evolutionary biology, University of Colorado, Boulder; Rick McIntyre, naturalist, wolf researcher, and author of nonfiction about wolves; Eduardo Fernandez-Duque, professor, Department of Anthropology and School of the Environment, Yale University; Christine L. Goforth, head, Citizen Science for the North Carolina Museum of Natural Sciences; Lisa Rapaport, behavioral ecologist and professor, Clemson University; Lauren Smith, director of communications, Owl Research Institute; Joaquín L. Navarro, professor and researcher, National University of Cordoba, Argentina; and Ray Tipper, bird photographer, author, and guide.

For Dave and George, two super devoted,
super silly, and super lovable dads
HL and JH

First edition 2024

Library of Congress Catalog Card Number 2023945064
ISBN 978-1-5362-1796-4

24 25 26 27 28 29 CCP 10 9 8 7 6 5 4 3 2 1

Printed in Shenzhen, Guangdong, China

This book was typeset in Futura.
The illustrations were done using traditional and digital collage.

Candlewick Press
99 Dover Street
Somerville, Massachusetts 02144

www.candlewick.com